HEART OF THE HORSE

HEART OF THE HORSE

PHOTOGRAPHS BY **JULIET VAN OTTEREN**
FOREWORD BY **JANE GOODALL**   TEXT BY **ALAN LIGHTMAN**

BARNES & NOBLE BOOKS
NEW YORK

To Iain McGarvie-Munn, my husband, friend, and collaborator.
His advice, help, and emotional support through this entire project from its
inception onward have been invaluable to me.

.

Foreword

*I*n this extraordinarily beautiful collection of photographs, Juliet van Otteren has captured perfectly the power and the grace and the fluid movements of horses. The images perfectly illustrate what Winston Churchill meant when he said "there is something about the outside of a horse that is good for the inside of a man." Each of these photographs is a precious fragment borrowed from a sequence, providing us with an intuitive understanding of the movements that preceded it and those that will follow. As we turn the pages, we have the illusion of experiencing the actual motions that inspired the photographs.

I have always known and loved horses, and looking through these pages has evoked powerful memories for me. At times I swear I could actually smell the tang of sweat-drenched hair, the rich odor of steaming dung, or the sweet fragrance of meadow grass as it is cropped by a grazing horse, plucking and crunching with strong lips and teeth. And I'm sure I heard, again and again, the thundering of galloping hooves, loud neighing, soft whickering, and gentle snorting. I hope such heightened awareness comes to you also.

When I was a child, we did not live in the country—nor could we possibly afford to have and care for a horse. Yet my childhood and adolescence were closely connected with horses and ponies. My aunt, who did live in the country, and had horses, gave me a reproduction of a Stubbs painting of a gray Arab called Arthur. I loved that painting, and have it still. I studied the paintings of the horses used in warfare in medieval times, ancestors of the shire horses and other pedigree draught horses, with their powerful haunches and shoulders, and thick necks tapering to tiny heads, bred to carry the weight of knights in armor. And I was fascinated to trace the fossil record, which shows how horses have evolved, over millennia, from little creatures about the size of a rabbit,

PLATE 3

to gradually bigger creatures, to the familiar forms of today's horses. Then there were the paintings of horses made by our Stone Age ancestors in the secret darkness of underground caves, images that look not unlike Mongolian wild horses and the ponies that still run free in England's New Forest and Dartmoor and Exmoor.

I first sat on a horse—a retired racehorse called Painstaker—when I was about two years old. He was owned by the brother of my horse-loving aunt. Then, about four years later during a holiday in the country, a round, plump, dappled gray pony called Cherry obligingly carried me round and round a field, teaching me balance and the "feel" of a horse.

For the rest of my childhood, horses were my passion. I spent almost every weekend, from the age of ten until I left school at eighteen, at a riding school that was part of a farm. I learned the elements of horsemanship on wise old Daniel, a black horse, going gray, who had once worked in a coal mine but had been rescued before he went blind. Then I graduated to a whole variety of mounts, many of them local New Forest ponies; my favorites were plump, somewhat placid Imp and canny, obstinate Chrysler. There was the dock-tailed cob called Peach, who jumped like a dream, and Blitz, who had been a milk pony and who had become blind in one eye, and Wellington, a magnificent bay who had survived duty in WWI pulling cannons. To the huge delight of those of us in the know, Wellington would take advantage of any new rider: he would lie down without warning and roll if he went through any kind of water, from a stream to a rain puddle. There were two thoroughbreds—Chance and her daughter Quince—whom I was eventually allowed to ride in horse shows, taking part in dressage and jumping (though it was not the ferociously competitive atmosphere of today's professional "horsey" world). Thus, because we could not afford a horse, I got to know many different horses and ponies, and learned from the beginning how different were their personalities.

For me, the real joy comes from knowing horses as individuals, each with his or her own character, likes and dislikes, skills and failings. This is why Juliet van Otteren's photographs are so moving to me. She has captured not only the grace and the controlled power of her subjects, but their emotions also. Indeed, I can see the very souls in the eyes of some of the individuals she has photographed. Do horses have souls? Well, if we do then I am sure they do, too.

Also, from my experience riding horses, I learned about the special, almost psychic, bond that can exist between horse and human. When I rode Painstaker at the age of two, I was able to guide him, all by myself, in figure eights in and out of the trees lining the side of the road. My aunt was amazed at what she considered my precocious skills, but what was really amazing was that this large horse allowed a very tiny child to guide him. Why? Was he intimidated by the adults in the vicinity? I think not. I think he felt a special bond with a child who loved him.

My own intuitive understanding of horses has stood me in good stead. When I arrived in Kenya and met my mentor, Louis Leakey, he told me that I could accompany him on a dig to the now famous Olduvai Gorge—*if his wife approved of me*. Imagine my state of nerves when I went to meet Mary! The occasion was a pony club "hunt." There was no killing involved—a person knowledgeable about the ways of the jackal (the usual substitute for a fox in colonial Africa) laid a scent trail. The young riders and their parents followed the hounds as best they could. Louis Leakey was as fascinating to the assorted onlookers as the riders themselves, for he had a conviction that his ancient Land Rover could negotiate the rough terrain, ditches and all, quite as well as dogs and horses! It was terrifying!

When the hidden prize had been located by the lavishly praised hounds, Louis led me over to Mary. She was standing holding the reins of her sturdy pony, Sherry, and she asked if I would like to ride him back to the house. No one told me that Sherry, when ridden by strangers, walked backwards, and that hours and hours had been spent vainly trying to cure him of this disconcerting habit. It was all part of the test, I suppose—like the hair-raising drive I had just survived. So I mounted, and Sherry, as usual, raced backwards, causing hilarity among those who knew him. Yet even when his idiosyncratic behavior was explained, I was sure something was wrong. Despite my nervousness of crossing Mary,

I insisted on dismounting and removing the saddle. And there was a large, red, and clearly painful saddle sore. After that I could do no wrong in Mary's eyes!

Of course, most of my life has been spent not with horses, but with chimpanzees. I've spent forty-four years learning about their behavior. They are more closely related to humans than any other animal, sharing approximately 99 percent of their DNA with us. They're capable of intellectual behaviors once thought unique to humans. They have emotions that are clearly similar to our own. They show compassion and altruism on the one hand, brutality and a form of primitive warfare on the other. They teach us that there is no sharp line dividing humans from the rest of the animal kingdom. We humans are not, as Western science and Western religion once insisted, the only beings on this planet with personalities, minds, and feelings. Many of us have always known this.

Yet when I got to Cambridge University in England to work for my Ph.D., I was told that, at least as far as science was concerned, the personalities, minds, and emotions of chimpanzees did not exist. Fortunately, I had been blessed with wonderful teachers throughout my childhood who had given me an intuitive understanding of the deeply individual emotional character of animals—my dog Rusty, and all the horses and ponies with whom I had spent so many wonderful days. And our cats, Figaro and Pickles, and two guinea pigs, Gandhi and Mrs. Jimmy. I also had come to know the sad inmates of the ape house in the London Zoo: the gorilla Guy, and the chimpanzees, Dick and his mate.

As a child I was deeply saddened and angered by cruelty to animals. I was appalled when I heard how so many old, sick horses, no longer useful to their owners, were exported alive to continental Europe to be killed and sold as horse flesh. My sister and I used some of our precious pocket money to join an organization called Cherry Tree Farm that bought such horses and provided them a safe haven for the rest of their lives. We used to go around with a tin collecting box and force our friends—and even strangers in the street—to donate. Sadly, the same barbaric practice continues today. And there are so many other cruelties to horses everywhere, from the beating of those condemned to pull or carry monstrously heavy burdens, to the cruel training of show jumpers and race horses. Add to that the rounding up and shooting or selling into servitude of wild mustangs, legacy of the Spanish invaders and the Plains Indians.

Together, we must try to bring such cruelties to an end. There is something especially tragic about the idea of these magnificent animals leading lives of pain and fear, ending their days forgotten and unloved. For horses have been part of human history since time immemorial, admired and celebrated by people all over the world.

I hope that this book, with its immensely powerful and moving images, will not only give enormous pleasure to the horse lovers who will want to own it and display it on their coffee tables, but that it opens the eyes and awakens the hearts of many who have never had the chance to fall under the ancient spell of the horse. In particular, I hope that more people will gain a sense of the horse's essential dignity and the freedom of its spirit.

I can think of no better way to end my statement, to lead into the following pages of stunning photographs, than with this ancient Bedouin legend of how horses came into being: "And God took a handful of southern wind, blew his breath over it, and created the horse."

Jane Goodall Ph.D., D.B.E.
Founder, The Jane Goodall Institute
U.N. Messenger of Peace
www.janegoodall.org
May 2004, Ridgefield, Connecticut

Introduction

*W*hen I travel, between my vehicle and me I prefer to be the only one thinking. In an early experience with a horse, I confidently mounted my vehicle and expected to command it with my heels and reins as if I were using the gas pedal and steering wheel of a car. Almost immediately, however, I realized that there was another mind working beneath me. My vehicle went galloping off in a direction not of my choosing, straight under the low-hanging branch of a tree. I was left sprawling on the ground to reconsider my concept of horses.

Throughout human history, the horse has held a special place among animals. A wall painting in the cave at Pech-Merle, France, dating from about 13,000 B.C., shows two spotted horses with beautiful curving backs and strong haunches. A chest from the tomb of Tutankhamen, about 1325 B.C., depicts a warrior riding in a chariot pulled by two horses, decorated with headdresses and rearing proudly on their hind legs. In the Trojan War, the treacherous gift of the Greeks was a giant wooden horse. The wily Greeks played upon the Trojans' love of horses. In Jonathan Swift's *Gulliver's Travels*, the most virtuous creatures that Gulliver meets are the horses, called Houyhnhnms.

The "noble Houyhnhnms are endowed with a general disposition to all virtues," including friendship, decency, and civility.

We are fascinated by horses. Horses are beautiful to look at, powerful and graceful at the same time, regal in bearing, intelligent, sensitive, spirited. For millennia, horses have carried warriors into battle or transported people between towns or helped farmers plow fields or provided affectionate companionship. Other horses remain wild and untamed, unbridled. Indeed, the very word "unbridled" has come to mean anything beyond our control. Thunder is also unbridled. But bridled or unbridled, horses speak to us if we listen. When standing beside a horse, we feel in the presence of a fine and noble spirit. We feel elevated.

In these extraordinary photographs, you will see horses as you've never seen them before. You will feel, you will imagine, you will travel to new places—both with the animals and within yourself. In the brief accompanying essays, I have tried to express my own journeys.

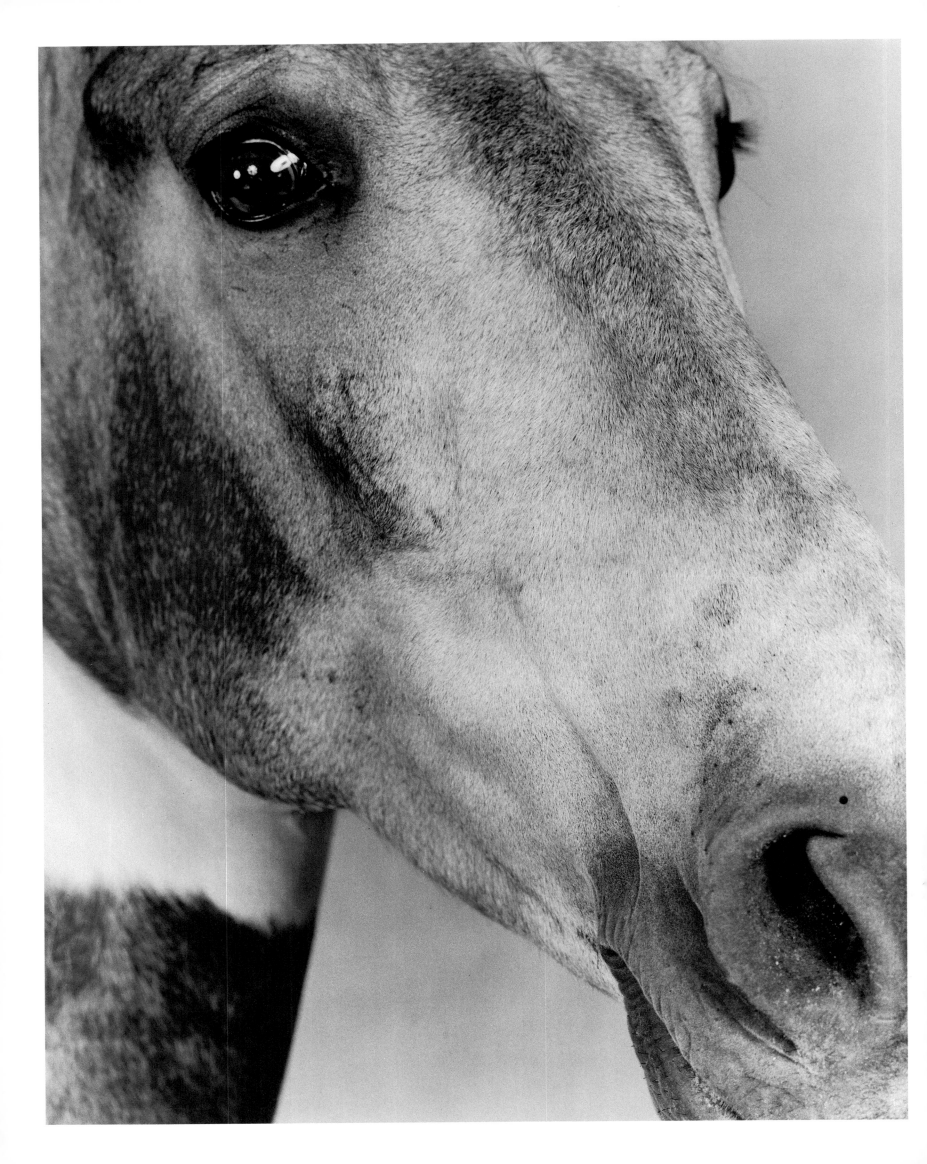

Portraits of Feelings

THESE HORSES GET INTO YOUR BODY. You find yourself fastened by their gaze. What kind of intelligence lies behind these eyes? What worlds of emotion? Continents wait. A gift has been given, and you want to give back.

Years ago, I had a dog who would seek me out whenever he was unhappy and begin howling. I might be reading, or washing dishes, or even sleeping in my bed. I'd always be startled. He'd plant himself several feet away, often stinking of garbage and wet fur, hang his head, and let out a long and sorrowful cry. If I moved to another room, he'd follow and continue to wail. Nothing would stop him except sympathy. Within a few minutes, I could usually tell if he was hurt, or hungry, or just plain starved for affection. His eyes told the story.

It was quiet where I lived at that time, so quiet that I could hear a train whistle a mile away. I would sometimes sit at the window, half asleep in the warm air and the silence. What sound was that? An ant dragging its body across the sill? The faint hum of the refrigerator downstairs? Or my own breathing. I would awaken from my afternoon daze and feel that I was talking without words to my dog. And he heard me, if anybody did. He would wag his tail or droop his eyes, tremble like a leaf in light wind to my hints of fear, pleasure, beauty, loneliness, mystery.

This is what you do with a dog. You feed it. You take it on walks in good weather, and bad. You stroke it. You apply gentle pressure to muzzle, back, paws, and other emotional surfaces. You sometimes lie on the floor with it. You leave lights on in certain parts of the house.

I still think of that old brown dog, especially in quiet moments. I remember his howl, forlorn, and the way that he looked at me as if I were his last friend in the world. I might be

PLATE 4

shaving at the mirror, staring at my reflection and hoping to see something new. And I recall the exchange of feelings I had with that animal. I recall the sensation of power, of being part of some larger world. With that animal, I moved outside of myself. At times, human language seems so paltry. At times, we seem to have abstracted ourselves into nothingness, marks on a page, or formal grunts. At times, our verbal contact with other people is like the narrow sliver of the electromagnetic spectrum that is visible to the human eye. Cats, dogs, horses pick up the infrared and the ultraviolet.

A friend of mine goes to meditation retreats, where no one speaks for three weeks. When he returns, he is sensitive as a cat. He knows how I am feeling from the slant of my body, the way that I fold my hands, my breathing. He is looking in from other wavelengths.

In the summer, I live on a small island in Maine. It's a skinny finger of land, several hundred feet wide and half a mile long, pointed northeast and southwest like the other islands in Casco Bay. When I go out in my boat and look at the island end-on, it doesn't appear as the tip of a finger but as a round dollop, with spruce trees sticking up from its crown like green bristly hair. A high ridge runs down the spine of the island, a hundred feet above sea level, and my house lies on the north end of the ridge. From there, the ocean is a stone's throw in all directions but south.

The island basks in its isolation and silence. There are no roads or bridges, no ferries, no telephone service, no fax machines, no electronic mail. The rest of the world is a light-year away. However, like Thoreau in Concord, I have traveled far and wide on the island. I know each cedar and poplar, each cluster of spruce, each clump of wild rose, *Rosa rugosa*, each patch of blueberry bushes and raspberry brambles and lush moss. Sometimes, I just sit in my house by a window, half asleep in the warm summer air, and listen to animal sounds.

Six or seven years ago, a family of ospreys built a nest about a hundred feet from my house. Since then, I have been watching their life cycles with great fascination. Ospreys are among the largest flying birds, with wing spans of several feet, and their nests are enormous. Ospreys are also monogamous. After spending separate vacations in South America or some other warm climate, the mother and father osprey return to the same nest, arriving within days of each other in the middle of April. The mother lays eggs and broods. By early June, the eggs hatch, usually two but sometimes three babies. The mother stays with the growing children while the father fishes and brings his catch back to the nest. Sometimes, they take turns and switch roles. By early August, the baby ospreys are pretty big, tan and spotted, and receive their first flying lessons. In the beginning, they get tangled up in trees upon landing, the mother loudly scolding with directions and the father grandly aloof in a nearby tree.

By the end of August, the young ospreys are expert fliers. Then, they leave the nest, to return a year or two later to the vicinity but not to the nest they grew up in. The parents fly away in the middle of September, take their separate vacations, return to the original nest in April, and lay eggs. And the cycle repeats.

Over the course of the years, I have learned the different calls of the ospreys and their meanings. A single, piercing chirp means that food is on its way. A series of high-pitched chirps followed by a low clucking sound means danger. I've heard a string of eight or ten squeals from the mother, aimed at her offspring in early August when she is trying to coax them to fly. Her children answer with a similar sound.

From the mother osprey, I've learned about patience, courage, and caring. I don't read these qualities from her face, but from her body movements and behavior. When her babies are still small, she covers them with her wings through all kinds of weather. One night, we had a vicious storm, with torrential rain and wind. Every now and then, I would look out from my dry house and see the dark silhouette of the mother, steadfastly protecting her brood while she was getting pummeled and drenched.

A few years ago, I had an astonishing experience with the young ospreys. I had been watching them all summer from my second-floor deck, which is shaped like a semicircle and about eye-level with the nest. For two months, as the young birds had been slowly maturing, still bound to their nest, they had been looking at me as I looked at them. To them, the circular deck of my house must have appeared as my nest.

In the middle of August, after several days of frustrated flapping, the two young ospreys began to fly. On the third day, they had gotten the hang of it and began cavorting in the air, chasing and dive bombing each other. On the following day, I was standing on my circular deck when the two birds spotted me as they flew over the bay. They changed course and flew straight at me. For some reason, I wasn't frightened, despite their large size, high velocity, and powerful claws. And they weren't afraid of me either. Like jet planes, they shot about five feet over my head and then made a steep turn upward to clear the roof of the house. Just before they passed over my head, they looked directly into my eyes. There was no mistaking it. We made eye contact. For a half second, we looked into each others' eyes.

After they had gone, I could not stop shaking. And I broke into tears. In that half second of eye contact, I felt that I was part osprey. I had known those ospreys since their birth. We had been watching each other for months, each from our own nest, living together on the same spit of land, and I believe the ospreys wanted to acknowledge that bond. We were brothers. That fleeting glance in the air was charged with mutual respect and love and a shared sense of life. I have rarely felt as deep a connection to a human being.

When I look at Juliet van Otteren's photographs, I feel that I am part horse.

PLATE 5

PLATE 6

PLATE 7

PLATE 8

PLATE 9
OVERLEAF: PLATES 10 AND 11

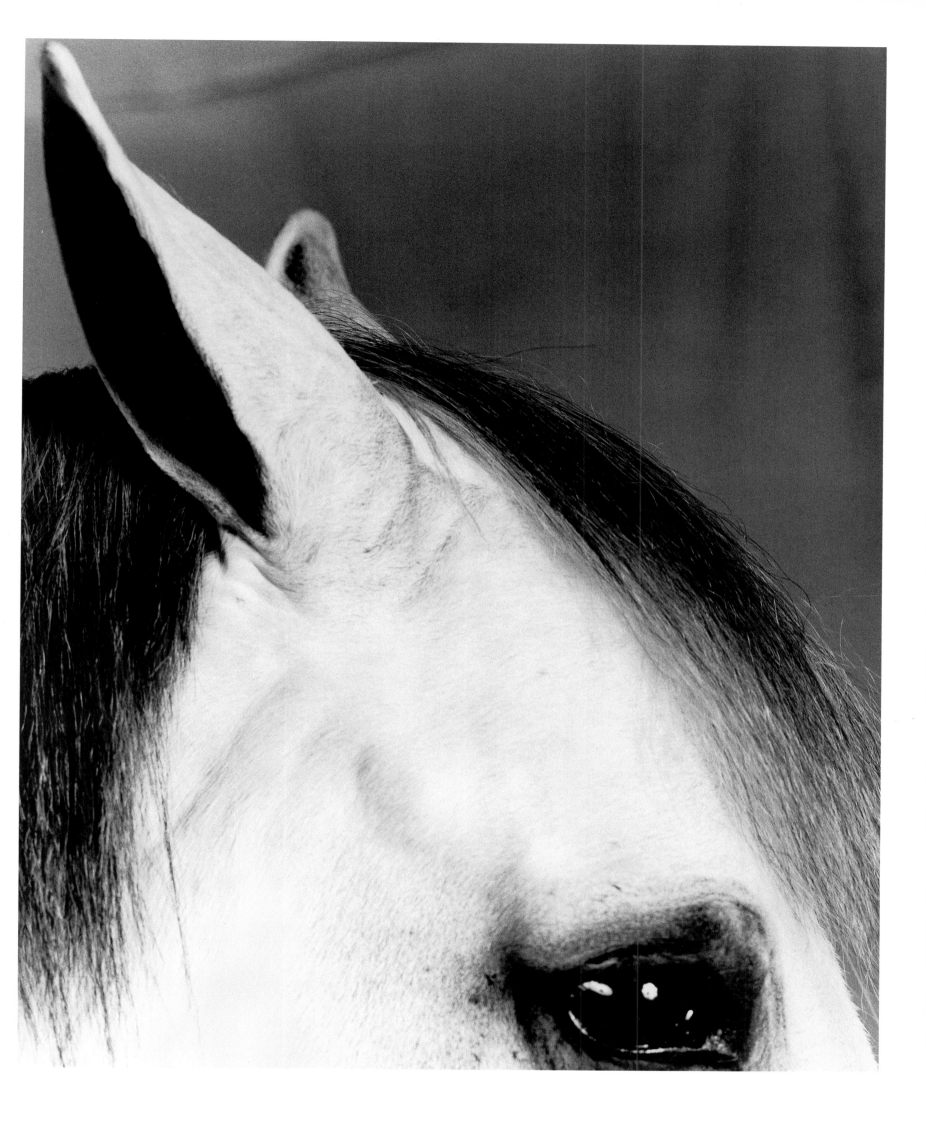

PLATE 12
OVERLEAF: PLATES 13 AND 14

PLATE 15
OVERLEAF: PLATES 16 AND 17

PLATE 18

PLATE 19
OVERLEAF: PLATES 20 AND 21

PLATE 22

Connections

IN ONE PHOTOGRAPH, TWO YOUNG HORSES jeer affectionately at each other. They must be siblings. One twists its head back toward the other in an angular thrust, opens its mouth wide to show teeth, and neighs. The other tosses its head up as if nodding to what's being said and stares down at its sibling. The first is the talker, the second the listener. They stand at ease, comfortable with their bodies and with this moment together. I've seen these two before—a couple at a restaurant sharing gossip as they wait for their meal; two children at the beach telling stories to each other while they play in the sand; two sibling ospreys flying side by side.

These horses are touching each other. They nuzzle, they smell each other, they glance into each other's eyes. They banter and play. Quite possibly, they slant their heads and torsos differently in groups than when alone. What new energy fills the air when two horses meet? What silent messages do they exchange? What needs are satisfied?

I once went on a camping trip in Yosemite National Park, in May. At the time, I needed to get away from a life of noise and speed and too many people. So I hiked into the park by myself, following a rambling trail through meadows, forests, ravines between mountains. Along the way, I saw gorgeous harlequin lupines, with their red, yellow, and pink petals hovering together like a congregation of butterflies. I saw western redbuds following the bank of a stream, pea-like pink flowers. I saw fields of waterfall buttercups, their white petals encircling green spiky crowns. The Pacific dogwoods were in bloom, with their creamy white flowers sprinkled on the branches like snow. And the mountains, towering over the meadows and

PLATE 23

valleys. I was in a cathedral. After several days of walking, I saw no one. I hiked up to high altitude, to the snow line, and pitched my tent at the base of a snow-covered mountain. I had food for another ten days.

I remember that tent, orange and nylon, a two-person tent, which made luxurious living for just me by myself. I was well stocked with mosquito netting, but few mosquitoes ventured to such high ground. A few metal stakes for securing the tent had been lost, a situation I remedied by carving wood stakes from the fallen limbs of trees.

At night, I rolled up in my goose-down sleeping bag and gazed at the stars. In those silent hours, I thought about the curve of my life, the places I had been and not been, mistakes made, hopes for the future, people I had loved in the past. The night sky was hard and luscious, and it received everything.

Each morning, I awoke at dawn. I would crawl out of my tent, shivering, start a fire for hot chocolate and bacon, and then watch as the air began to glow brighter, as if it were slowly filling up with blood. The series of peaks, slopes, and jags, dimming to purple in the distance, were like the bony back of some giant sleeping animal. And if I listened carefully, I could hear the animal breathing, a low sighing sound. In the early morning, the snow on the mountains looked like a soft blue cloth. Turning to lower elevations, I could see beige forests, I could see great swaths of green. From time to time, a deer would wander by, noiseless and dignified, stare at me for a few moments, and then disappear.

I was alone with the beauty. At first, I cherished my solitude. But after a while, it began suffocating me. The beauty had become too intense to absorb by myself. I needed to share it. The mountains and the snow and the trees and the glowing air had filled me beyond the point where I could hold it all in.

Too much had been created in me. I needed another human being to whom I could say: This moment is life. This moment is being alive. Do you also see these mountains, these trees, this air? Or am I imagining it all? Do you also hear the crunching sound of your footsteps in the snow? Can you touch this hand, my hand? Or am I imagining myself? Do you have memories, like me, of cold mornings, of certain houses, of certain people you have loved?

Having gone to the park for isolation, I became desperate for company. I packed up my tent and hiked out. I needed to pour myself into another person.

A few years later, when I went off on my honeymoon, I had the good sense to take my wife along. We chartered a sailboat and traveled between the islands of Greece. It was just the two of us. On the last day, we sailed from Hydra to Piraeus, a distance of about forty miles. Because the wind was at our backs, we didn't need to tack or fuss with the trim. We just let out the sails all the way, cleated the lines, and were catapulted at great speed through water and air, our destination slowly growing from an invisible speck beyond the horizon to a squirming seaside town. During the eight hours of the voyage, my wife and I said nothing to each other. Yet we shared every moment of exhilaration, every thought, every change in the color of the sea.

Touch, physical contact between animals, seems to be essential to maintain equilibrium. Researchers have shown that chimpanzees who are not cuddled and touched as babies later go nearly insane. Human beings who grow up with little social contact become mentally ill. A recent example is "Genie," the California woman whose father kept her imprisoned by herself in a small bedroom until age thirteen, when she finally escaped. With few words said to her as a child, Genie never developed complete language. More disturbing, she has never gained much social awareness. Alone or in a group of people, her emotions burst out unexpectedly in tantrums, sudden laughs, screams, as if she lives in a world of her own.

A famous test of whether a computer has achieved "intelligence" involves putting the machine on one side of a curtain and a human being on the other. The human types questions and comments on a keyboard, and the computer answers, with its responses appearing on a screen. In this way, the computer and the person have a conversation. If the human cannot guess whether a computer or another human sits on the other side of the screen, then the computer is deemed "intelligent." Most likely, the computer HAL in Stanley Kubrick's *2001* would pass such a test.

For me, this hypothetical experiment only underscores the difference between artificial intelligence and communication. For me, communication is physical—it requires the presence of two living beings. Words need not be spoken. Sounds need not be uttered. A world can be shared in a glance, a touch, a shake of the head. The noiseless exchange between two people, or two dogs, or two horses involves pathways so delicate and numerous and ultimately unfathomable that I doubt they could ever be reduced to the megabits of a computer or the language of words. What is being exchanged? Life.

Sometimes, when I despair of the shortness of life, I consider the possibility that we are not individual creatures with individual minds, each of us arriving and departing one by one like the flickering of fireflies, but rather that we may all be part of one living being, a single mind and a single passion, extending from centuries in the past to centuries in the future. In this view, when we look at each other, we are looking at ourselves. When we touch each other, we are touching ourselves. When we think a thought, we are thinking together. I believe that we have little choice. We must live with other lives to complete our own lives. We must touch others in order to be in touch with ourselves. We must be part of others, in order to be.

PLATE 24

PLATE 25

OVERLEAF: PLATES 26 AND 27

PLATES 28 AND 29

PLATE 30
OVERLEAF: PLATE 31

PLATE 32

PLATE 33

PLATES 34 AND 35

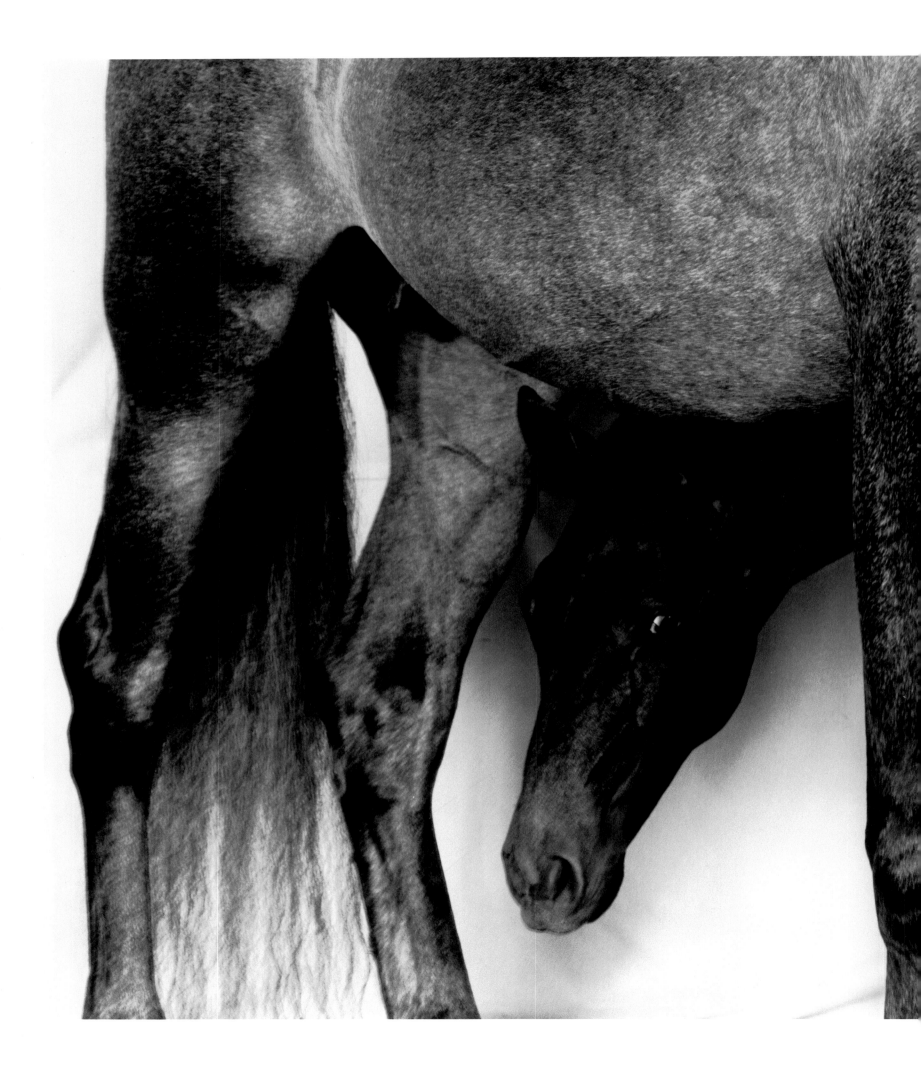

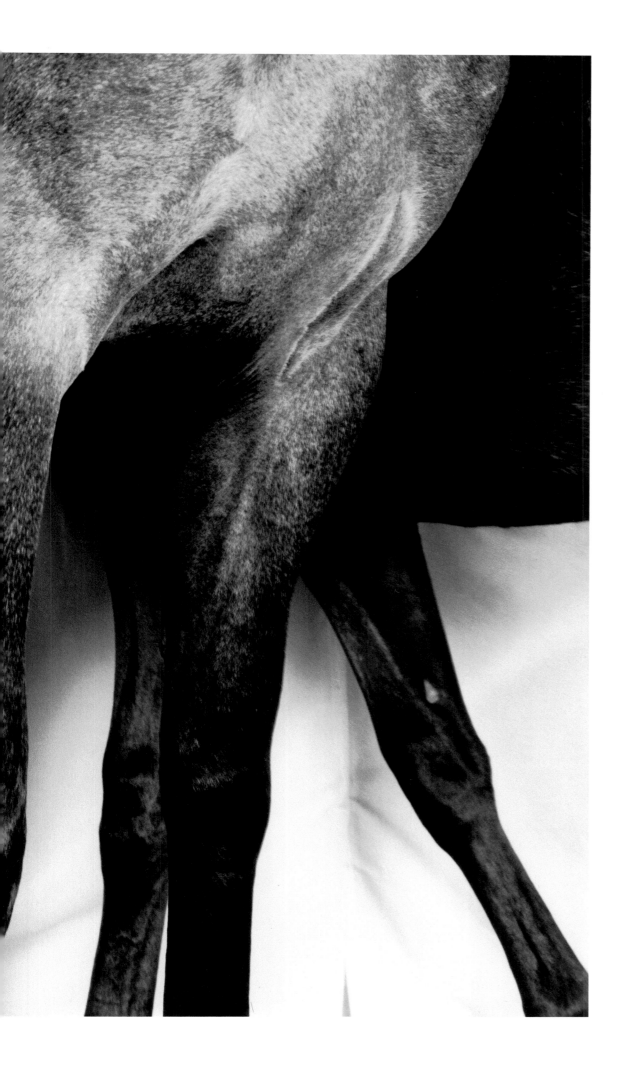

PLATE 36

PLATE 37
OVERLEAF: PLATE 38

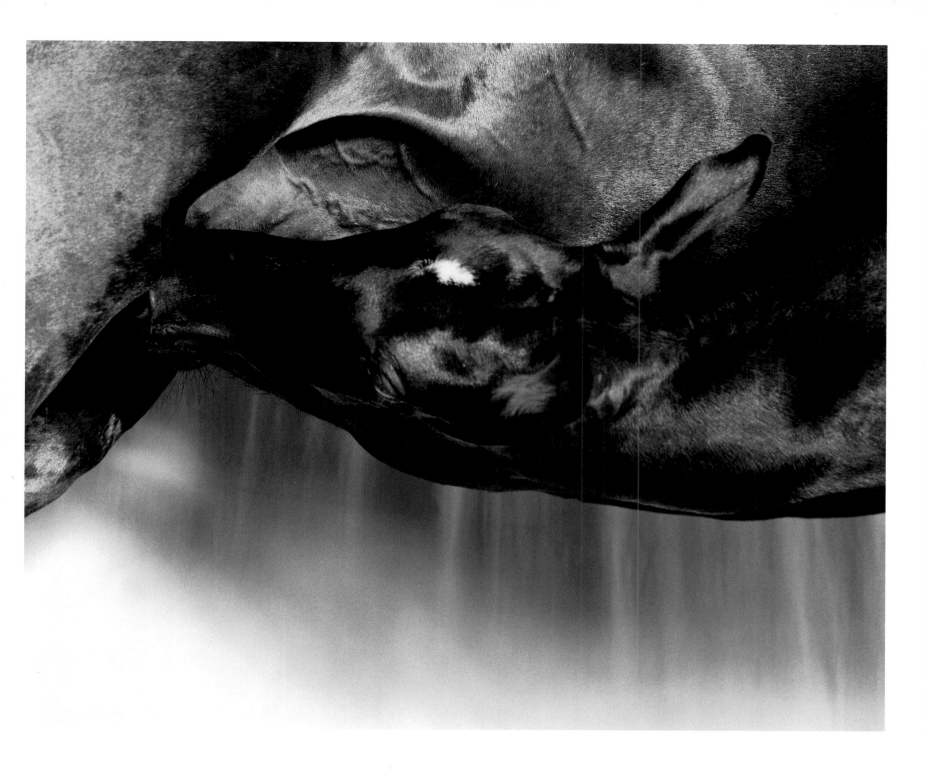

Motion

CAN MOTION BE FROZEN IN TIME? Like a raindrop hanging in air, a pendulum cocked in mid-swing. A sentence half said. A horse reared up on its hind legs. A photograph. Can motion be frozen in time?

Imagine a horse galloping around a track. Legs move back and forth, rise and fall. The head jerks this way and that, the tail billows, a fine auburn dust spreads in the air.

Now, imagine only the first half of the lap. Less distance is covered in less time. Still, we see the legs thrashing, the mane flutter, the wild look in the eyes. Dissect the gallop again. Reduce it to a quarter lap, an eighth lap, a sixteenth, and on, ad infinitum, sectioning distance and time into smaller and smaller amounts, like a paragraph of fewer and fewer words, or a hunger of smaller and smaller domain. What remains?

The flight of our horse dwindles from a half mile to yards, to feet, to inches, to fractions of an inch—occupying seconds, then fractions of a second, then fractions of those fractions. The full gallop decreases to the once only clap of four legs. Then three legs, then two, then one. As parcels of distance and time diminish to nothing, our horse becomes frozen, its body caught in an infinitesimal action, its body fixed at one place and one time.

And yet, it moves. Its legs tilt gracefully in space. Its neck arches. Shadow and light trace the lines of its flexed muscles. Frozen in motion, it creates time without time.

If motion can be frozen in time, can light? The watery sunlight that flows through a field, creating the green luminescence of leaves, shining air, shadows littering the ground around trees—can this light be halted in time? Would leaves, air, shadows exist without the movement of light? Consider: light travels through space, reflects from objects, enters the eye of an

PLATE 39

observer, produces electrical currents in nerves that create certain sensations in the mind. If this journey were halted, would landscapes appear? Scenes might be compressed to single images, mere moments of perception that would instantly fade, since no new vibrations of light would move through the eye, or the mind. Only memories of scenes would remain—memories of trees, leaves, air, undulating hills. Such memories might or might not suffice.

If motion can be frozen in time, can love? In a room with a bed, a little pine writing desk, a turquoise porcelain lamp, light oozing around the slats of a shuttered window, can love be frozen in time? He holds the letter of his anguish, clasps and unclasps his hands, walks to her as she sits on the bed. His shoes tap faintly on the wood floor. Which of his movements is necessary? Which can be dispensed with? She grasps his wrist. He will forgive her, he says, his body inhaling the lavender scent of her skin, he must forgive her, for she is the only one who sees into him. Outside, the faint groan of a car, the clinking of glass bottles. She unbuttons one button of his shirt cuff. Her hair shifts slowly across her shoulders. Which of her movements is necessary? If she held rigid, or he, without moving, without speaking, what would they mean to each other? Or if she did not touch his face as she does now, trace her fingertips along the contours of his chest, if her hand traveled less widely across the mesas of his body, moved less and less distance until it moved not at all, became stranded in space and in time, would passion remain? Or if he did not follow the soft parts of her flesh with his lips, the hollow at the base of her neck, the slight swell of her belly, her breasts, if his lips were captured and held prisoner at one place and one moment, would she know his desire?

Without movement, could she remember the first time they met? Could she remember the public reading room that late night, glowing with scattered table lamps like ships on a dark sea, his asking her directions, the way that he looked in her eyes? And without movement, could he remember the checkerboard floor, the way that she wrinkled her nose when she laughed, her brilliant remarks? Could he remember their trip to the airport, when they had nowhere to go but simply sat in the car and watched the planes arrive and depart?

Perhaps memory is not possible without motion. Or perhaps memory, all history of past places and events, is present in each moment of time, so that one moment, although frozen like the raised leg of a horse or the waiting caress of a lover's hand, contains all of life. For memory may be another form of motion, and if motion can be frozen, then perhaps memory as well.

And if motion can be frozen in time, can thought? If bodies do not move against each other, if bodies are halted in time, can minds move? Can thoughts of passion, desire, love, ambition make their mysterious microscopic journeys without time? What terrain do thoughts need? A terrain of the body, a terrain of time?

He holds her. He places his head against her chest and listens to each beat of her heart, a movement of sorts, a motion that divides space into sections. The pine writing desk, the porcelain lamp unlit, the scattered clothes on the floor become fragments and fragments of fragments. The volume of the room is apportioned into cubes of ever-decreasing size. Likewise, the beating of her heart parses out time as the fragments of space or the seconds between ticks of the clock on the table. With decreasing measure, his thoughts must gather themselves up to fit between two beats of her heart, a fulcrum of thought, a point of intensity as bright as a sun.

And she, lying in his arms, imagines a horse galloping about a track. She imagines the feel of the air rushing by, the smell of wet grass, the twitching of muscles, the pants. She imagines gravity and speed. For motion can exist in the mind. And the beating of her heart can cut that motion into smaller and smaller splinters, until she has a single frame in her mind, a single equestrian moment of speed and grace, passion, love, and desire. One image. That single frame moves even though it does not move, creates time without time. That horse, fixed in its passion, is her passion.

And I, sitting at my own desk, imagine her as she imagines the horse. While time and space are repeatedly sectioned into smaller amounts, while my thoughts spiral in ever-decreasing circles, I see her in the room with her lover, I see the horse, I see the track, I see the segments of distance and time diminishing to nothing. I see, finally, the raised hoofs conquer gravity. I see pure motion and life. And I feel my own thought swirling in smaller and smaller circles, the movements of my hand as I write crossing less and less space, until I can write only this sentence, this word, one dot.

PLATE 40

PLATE 41

PLATE 42

PLATE 43

OVERLEAF: PLATES 44 AND 45

PLATE 46
OVERLEAF: PLATES 47 AND 48

PLATE 49

PLATE 50

PLATE 51
OVERLEAF: PLATES 52 AND 53

PLATE 54

PLATE 55

Sight Beyond Sight

I AM A BLIND MAN. I SEE ONLY lights and darks, I see only emptiness and fullness, rounding and angle. Textures I feel and imagine. I am a blind man. Worlds shift and tilt under my blind gaze. Worlds become other worlds.

These filaments of hair of the tail of a horse turn into the branching of frost crystals on a glass windowpane, which turn into the tributaries of a river running through low country, which become shards of glass from a shattered vase. These patches of black on the white underbelly become ink spreading on a white page, which becomes dark footprints in the snow, which become blackbirds in flight in a light sky, which become questions arising in an undreaming sleep. These eyes, burning and blurred, become dark islands in a sea, become two pomegranates on fire, become two galaxies in orbit light-years away. This curve of black neck against a speckled gray torso is yin and yang.

I am a blind man. I am straining to see. For me, the universe is reduced to shapes, curves and lines, suggestions of shadows. Like the categories of Plato, or the axioms of Euclid's geometry, the universe is reduced to its most basic forms.

Give me a curve, a straight line, a white, a black, and I will create. Chairs, tables, flowers, leaves, ships, rain, mountains, fish. I can divide space into these things: the space that is chair and the space that is not chair, the space that is rain and the space that is not rain. The space of the known and the space of the unknown.

But these are only perceptions, perhaps even illusions. For what we call chairs, rain, mountains, horses may be only particular arrangements of shapes as experienced from a particular perspective at a moment in time. And shapes can deceive the eye, or the mind.

PLATE 56

I look at my wife brushing her hair. We are in a second-floor room of the old house. A

curving banister, a wood floor. A Chopin sonata floats from downstairs like a breeze coming

through an open window. In the next room, her easel against the wall, her sticks of colored

pastels, jars of gouache, shelves of fiber paper. I know this woman. We are recently married.

I know the shape of her face, I know the curve of her body, I know the slow rise and fall of her

arm as she strokes her long hair. I know these shapes, these lines. I know the Billie Holiday

song that she softly sings. As she stands in front of the mirror, I stand behind her, watching

this woman I know, watching as her face brightens and dims with the passing of clouds and

the afternoon sun.

In a flicker of time, I look at my daughter brushing her hair. She stands in the same place,

in a second-floor room of the old house, the same curving banister, the same Chopin sonata or

perhaps a Ginastera danza floating from downstairs. Do details matter? She has the same long

hair, the same slow rise and fall of her arm. As she stands in front of the mirror, I stand watching

behind her. I remember her first wobbly ride across the lawn on her new two-wheel bike.

I look at her brushing her hair. At this moment, the image has changed from my wife to

my daughter without change—with no change of lines, of curves, of shadows and light. Or

perhaps the angles and patterns have changed imperceptibly. Alternatively, the same lines,

the same curves, the same lights and darks might equally make daughter or wife. In which

case, the world lies in the mind. In the mind, in sight beyond sight, the woman in front of me

brushing her hair may be either wife or daughter, displaced in time. In a similar way, the tail

of a horse may be the branching of frost crystals on a glass windowpane, or the winding

tributaries of a river flowing through low country, or the shards of glass from a shattered vase.

The burning and unfocused eyes may be dark islands, or pomegranates on fire.

Maybe it is only I who have changed as I stand watching my wife or my daughter brushing

her hair. Should I dare speak? Should I dare challenge this magical uncertainty of shadow and

light? Should I ask a question? If parts of my life have become other parts, just as the filamentary

tail of a horse changes to branching crystals of frost, should I know which thing exists at this

moment of time? Should I know which part of me exists now? Perhaps all possibilities exist simultaneously. If so, then this moment is both present and past. And it may not be possible to know if I have myself changed, because I am both what I once was and what I am now.

With all possibilities existing at once, wives and daughters, tails of horse and crystals of frost, all possibilities suggested by shadows and light—then all things become abstractions. That is, all things cease to have definite names. Chairs, tables, flowers, leaves, ships, rain, mountains, fish can be whatever we want them to be. Names become only suggestions of certain ways of seeing the world. In fact, names might be eliminated entirely. Then, when we look at a picture or scene, we would not be able to say: here is a chair, there is a ship, here is a drop of rain. We could say only that here is a particular curve, there is a dark or a light.

In a sense then, these photographs of horses—these filaments of tails, these eyes blurred and on fire, these loose flowing necks—contain the universe. And the universe curves back on itself, distills itself and intensifies and repeats. So that we finally come back to the horse, the pure essence of horse. The horse in all of its meanings and forms. Even without names, even without focused images, we feel the horse underneath. We feel the spirit and the heart of the horse.

PLATE 57

PLATE 58

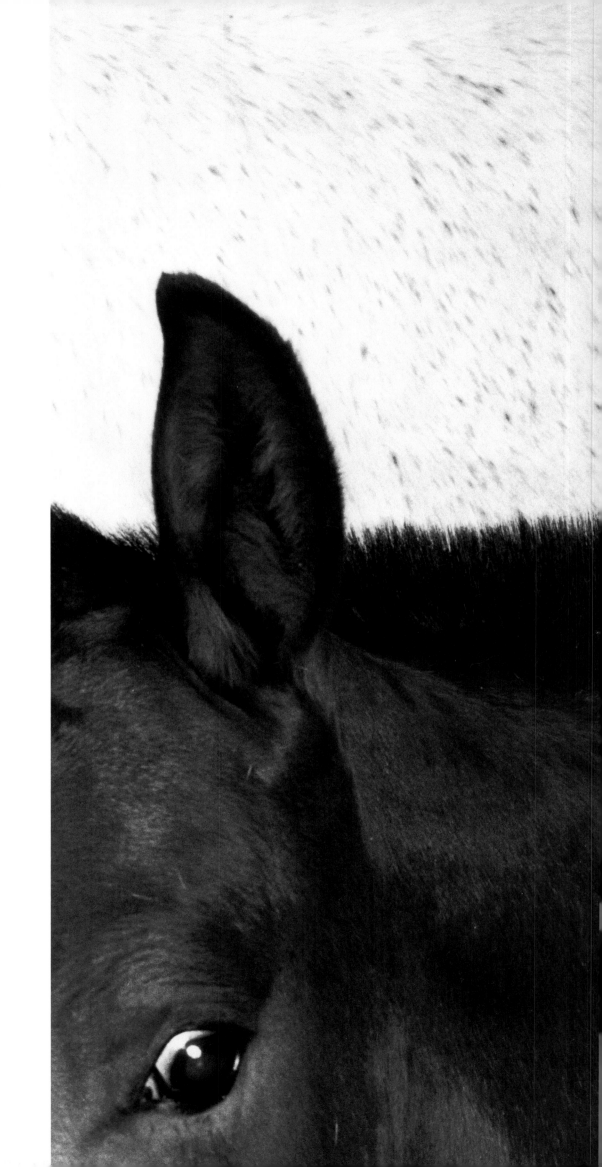

PLATE 59

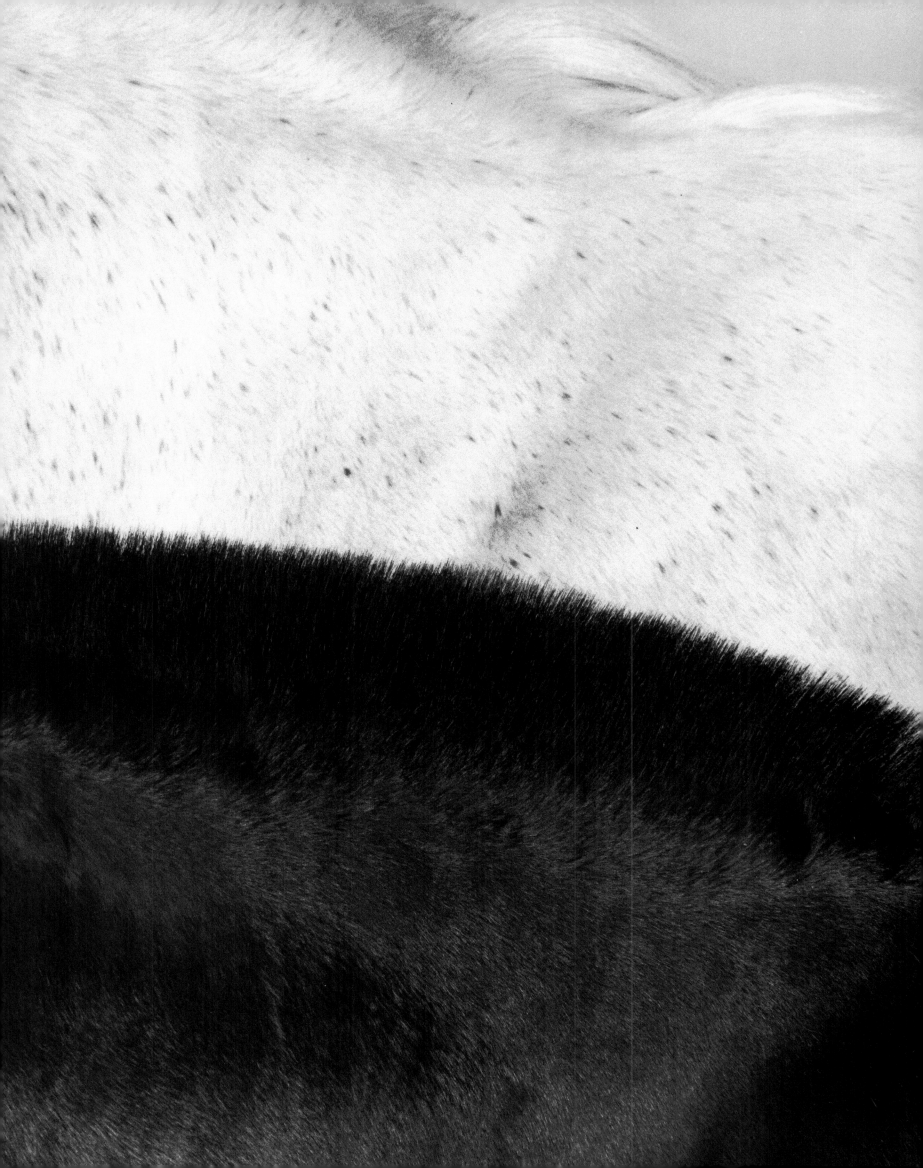

PLATE 60

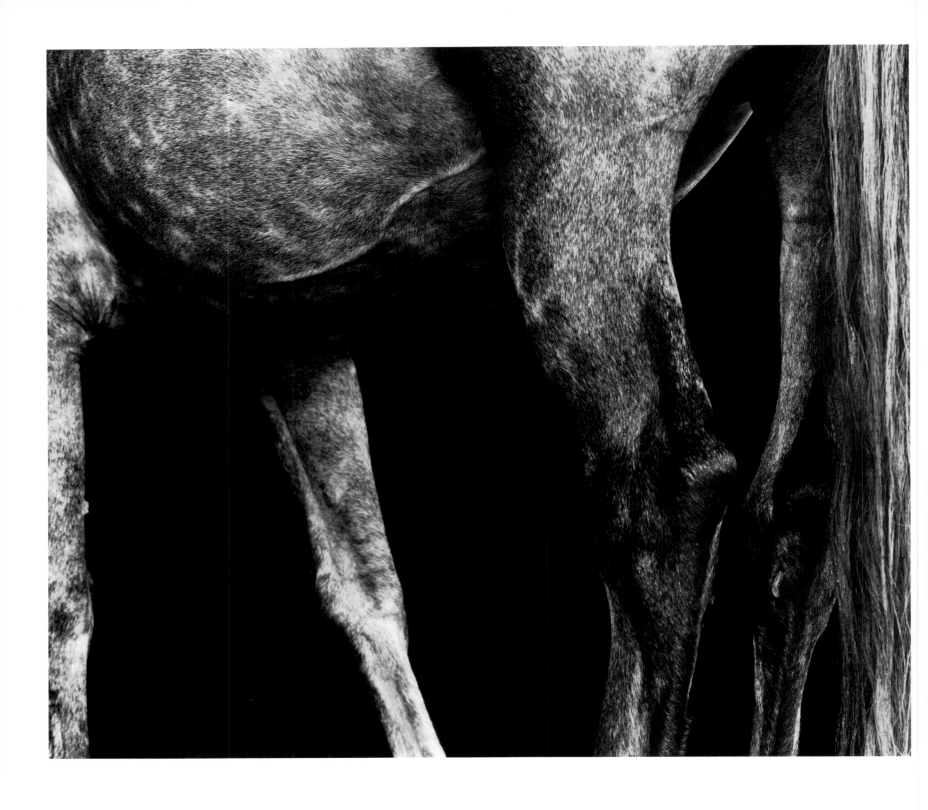

PLATES 61 AND 62
OVERLEAF: PLATES 63 AND 64

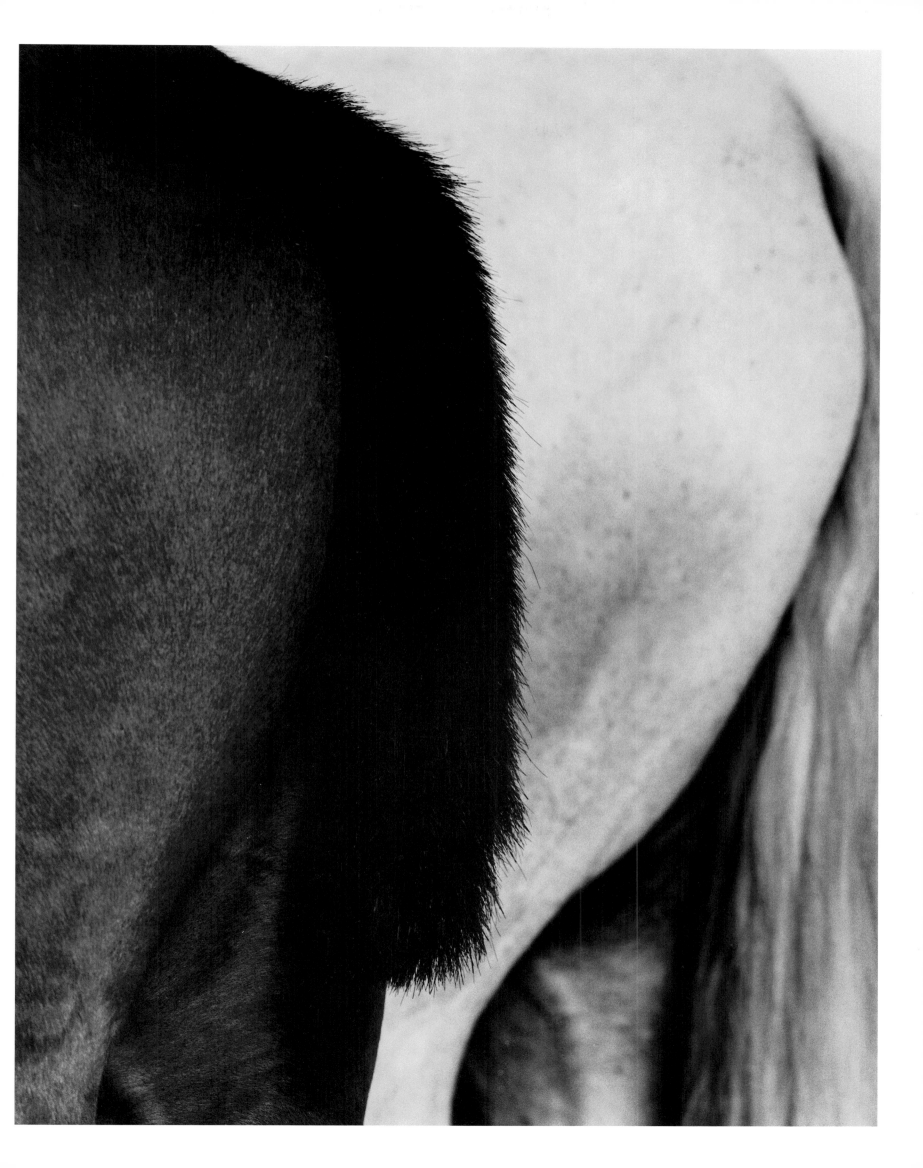

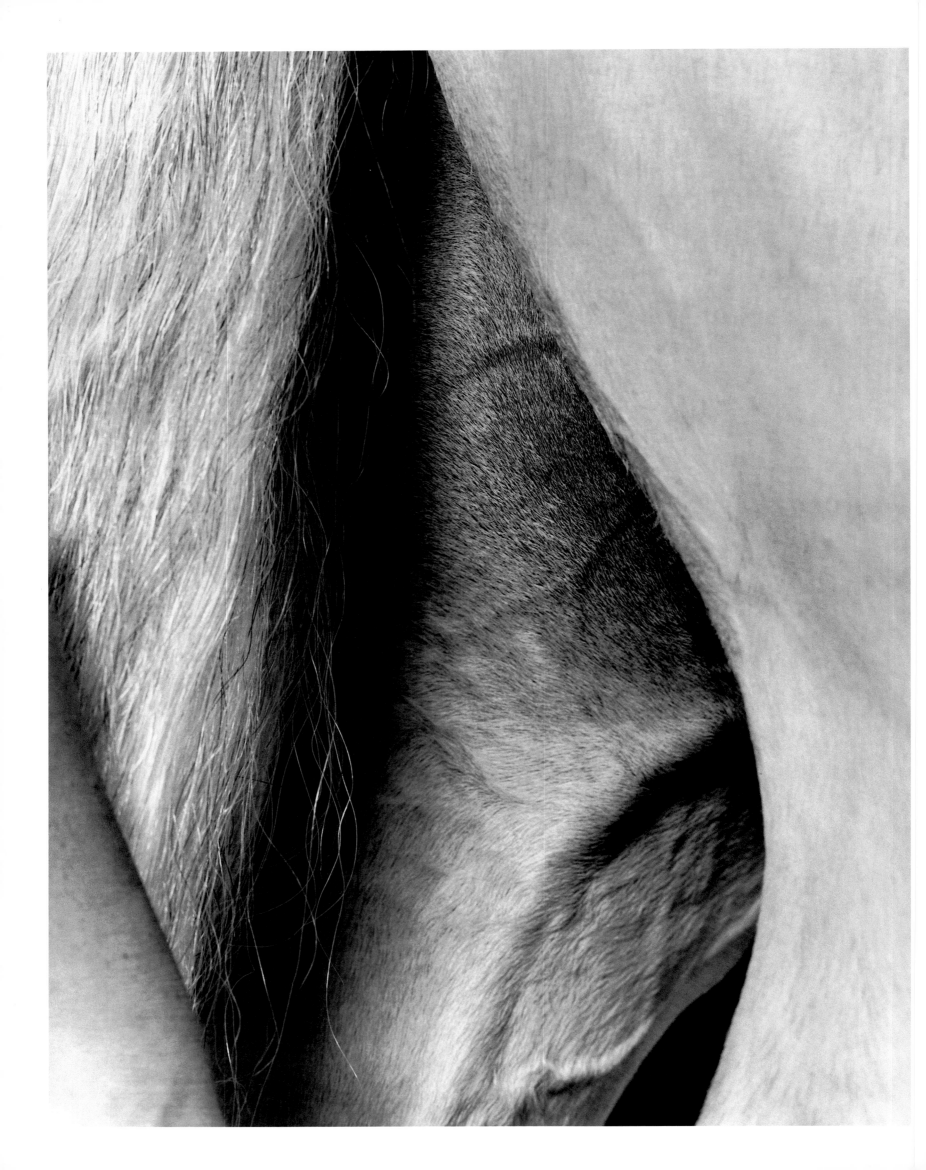

PLATE 65

OVERLEAF: PLATES 66 AND 67

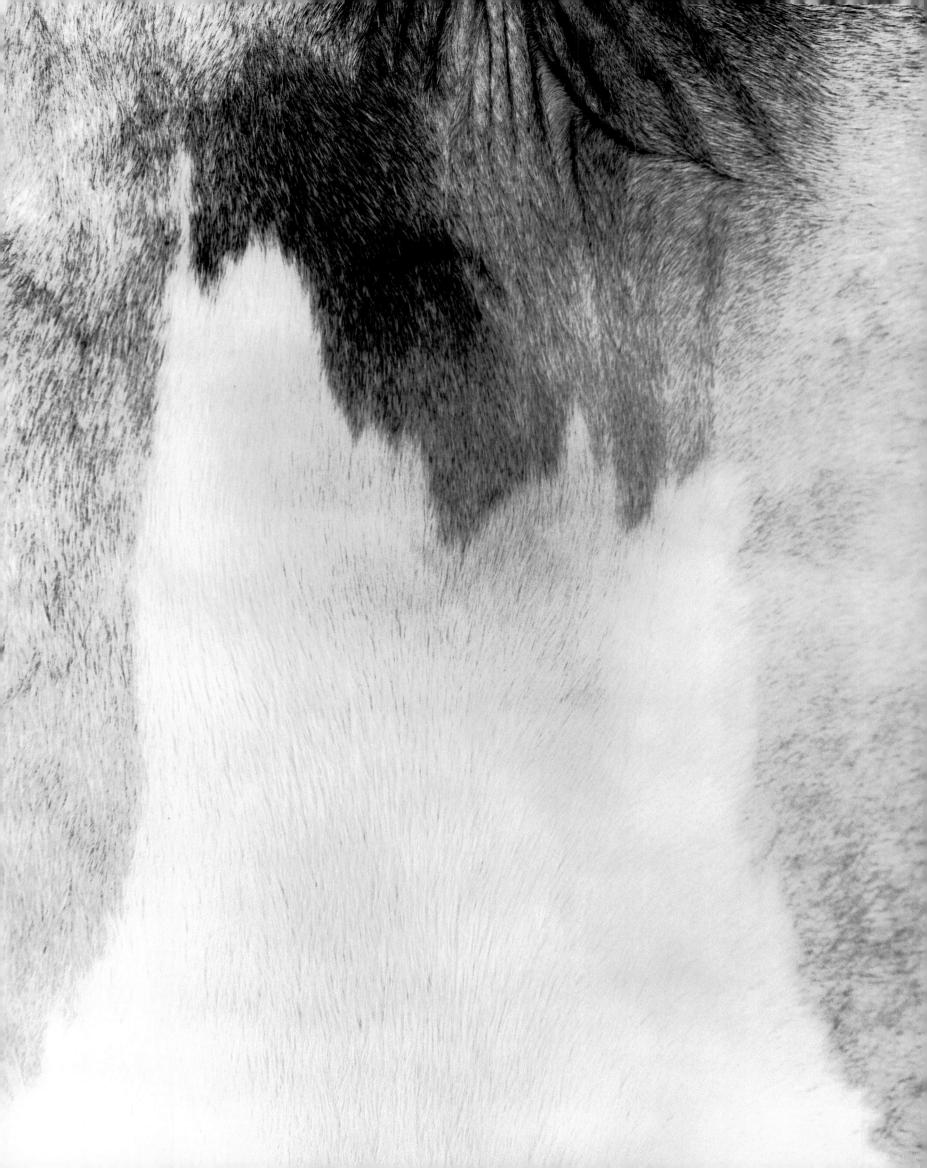

PLATE 68
OVERLEAF: PLATES 69 AND 70

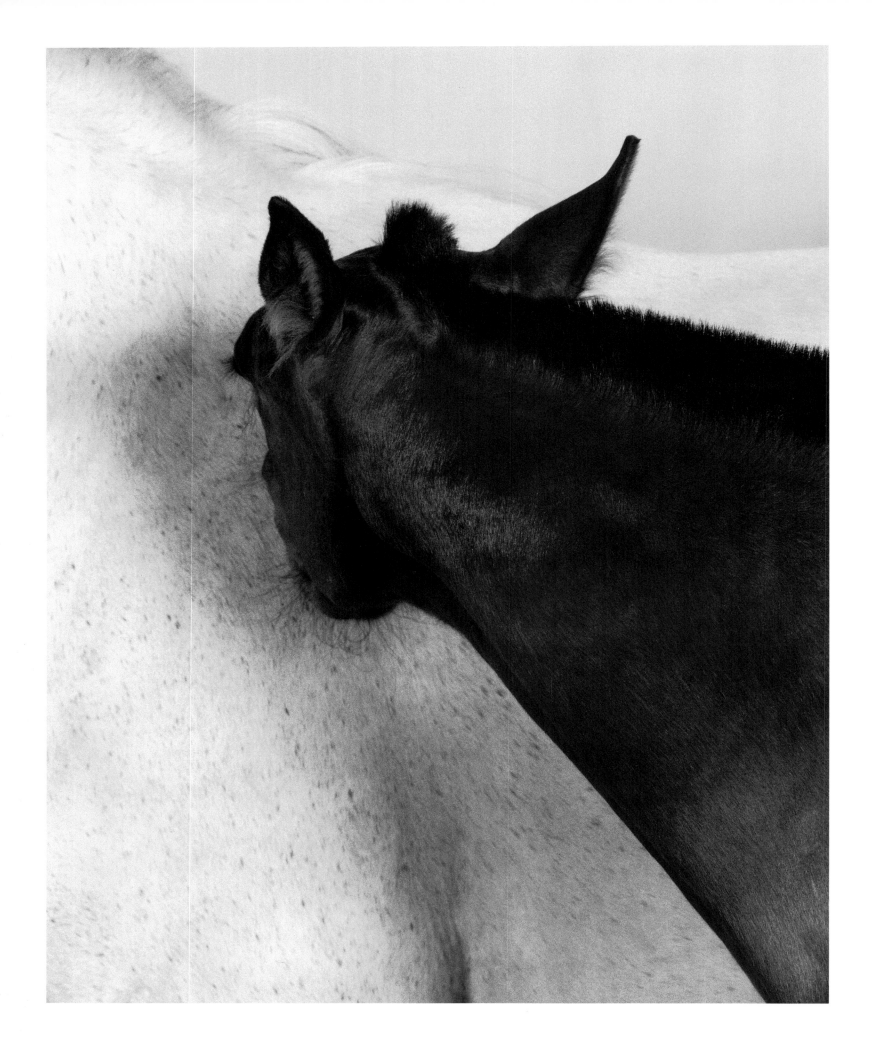

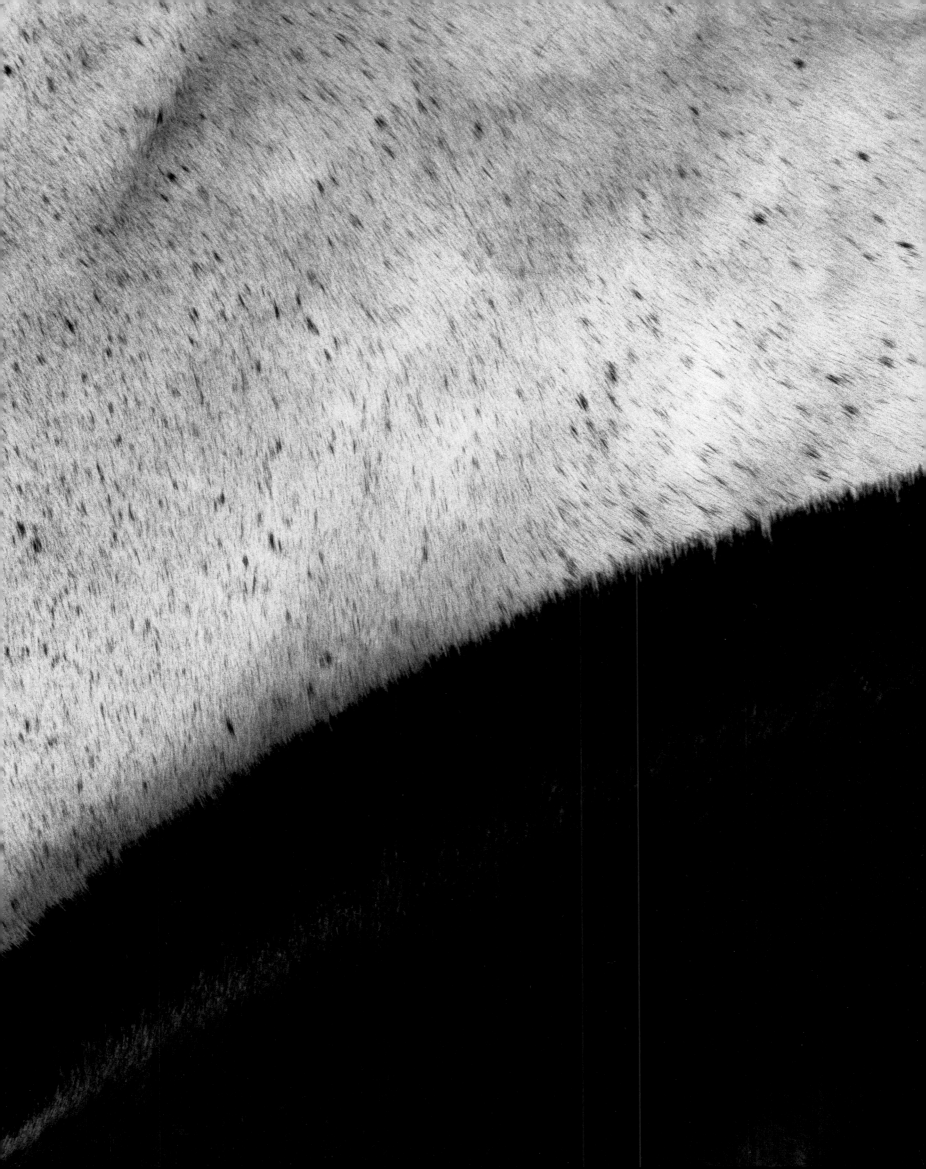

PLATE 71
OVERLEAF: PLATE 72

PLATE 73

PLATE 74
OVERLEAF: PLATES 75 AND 76

PLATE 77

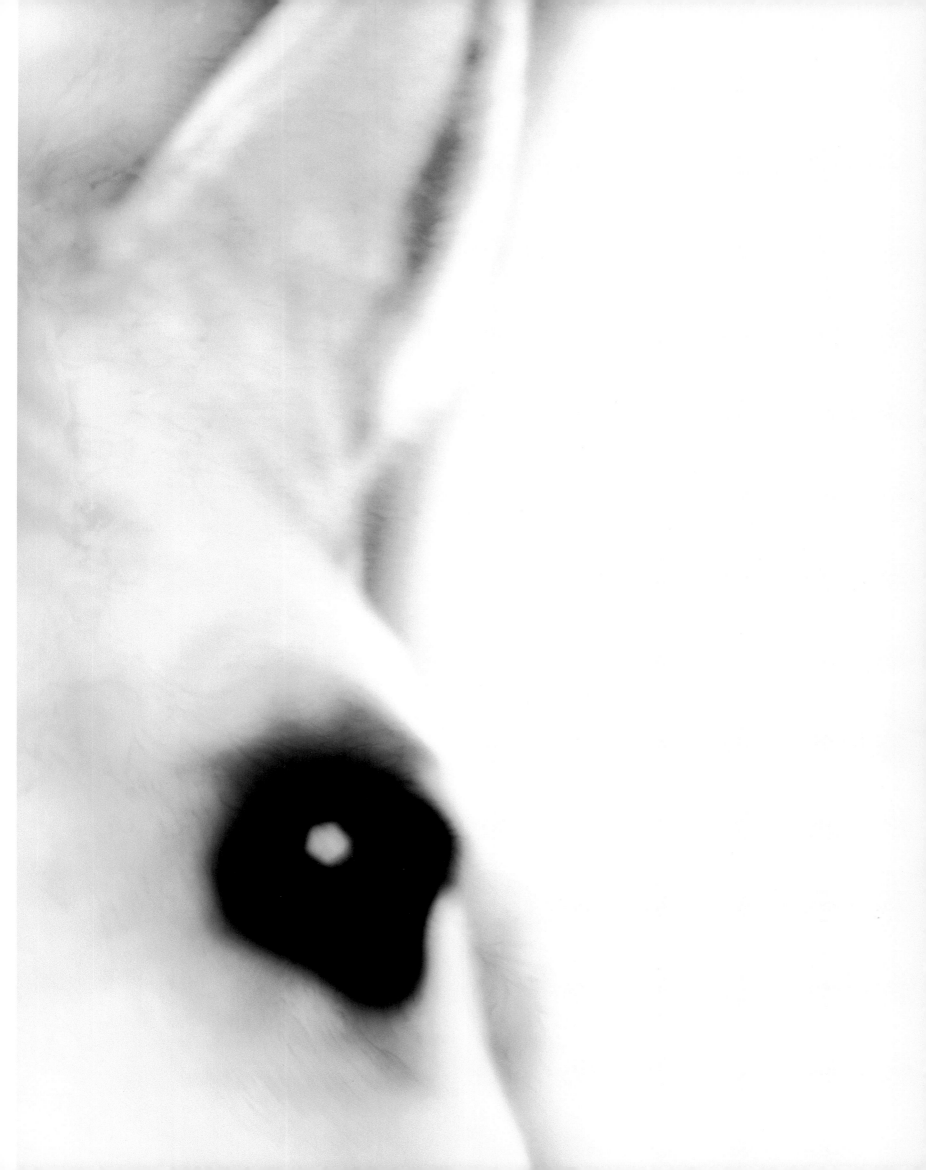

LIST OF PLATES

The photographs in this book are reproductions of limited edition 16" x 20" silver gelatin prints,
which have not been digitally altered or retouched.

Plate 1 Freedom—Escorial

Plate 2 Joy—Uther

Plate 3 Calm Repose—Uther

Portraits of Feelings

Plate 4	Soulfulness—Escorial
Plate 5	The Heart of the Horse—Uther
Plate 6	Contemplation—Uther
Plate 7	Samurai—Uther
Plate 8	The Shadow Self—Regaliz
Plate 9	Into the Mind—Uther
Plate 10	All About Uther 1—Uther
Plate 11	All About Uther 2—Uther
Plate 12	Vanity—Uther
Plate 13	A Quiet Moment—Uther
Plate 14	Melancholic—Uther
Plate 15	Wisdom—Escorial
Plate 16	Playfulness—Escorial
Plate 17	The Jester—Escorial
Plate 18	Humor—Uther
Plate 19	Death Mask—Uther
Plate 20	Frivolity—Regaliz
Plate 21	Passion—Regaliz
Plate 22	Dignity—Regaliz

Connections

Plate 23	Duet—Uther and Escorial
Plate 24	When I Was at the Waldorf—Uther and Escorial
Plate 25	Moulin Rouge—Uther and Escorial
Plate 26	Family Dynamics 1—Senta and Manrico
Plate 27	Family Dynamics 2—Senta and Manrico
Plate 28	Family Dynamics 3—Senta and Manrico
Plate 29	Family Dynamics 4—Senta and Manrico
Plate 30	Cityscape—Costosa and Manrico
Plate 31	The Nuzzle—Uther and Escorial
Plate 32	Stallions—Sharlamane and Evening Victory
Plate 33	Play Acting—Soldier and Felipe de Sourie
Plate 34	Tenderness—Augusta and Senta
Plate 35	Mother and Son—Costosa and Manrico
Plate 36	Curiosity—Costosa and Manrico
Plate 37	Nurturing—Bandit and Wolfram
Plate 38	Boy Games—Sharlamane and Evening Victory

ACKNOWLEDGMENTS

FIRST, I WOULD LIKE TO SINCERELY THANK Mike Fine for introducing me to Alan Kahn. I'm especially grateful to Alan for having had the vision to pursue *Heart of the Horse.*

I wish to commend my parents, Helen and Bud, for the patience they showed for my "horse obsession," and I thank them both—my father for his generosity in buying me my first horses and my mother for endlessly driving me to the stables.

My heartfelt gratitude also goes to:

— Alan Lightman, for his subtle, deeply insightful, gorgeous prose. Alan, thank you for writing the words I felt in my heart.

— Jane Goodall, my first icon, for honoring me with such a deeply moving and personal foreword. I'm still in awe of the extraordinary work she does for animals the world over, and for the message of peace she carries with her. Thanks to Mary Lewis for communicating my project to Jane.

A special thank you to the kind and wonderful people who allowed me to work with their horses, whom they treat with love and respect:

— Sarah Hollis, holistic horse trainer and breeder, owner of Tintagel Enterprises, Ltd., whose open-hearted and receptive horses were a joy to photograph: Regaliz, Bandit, Costosa, Encina, Escorial, Manrico, Operista, Pamina, Senta, Wolfram, and the great Uther, who was my inspiration for this book. I spent many days at Tintagel, where Sarah shared with me her methods of communicating with these amazing beings. She taught me that I too could communicate with horses as well as with all animals. But it was the great Uther who convinced me of this when, one day during a shoot, he placed himself in a complicated position simply because I was thinking about what a great photo it would make!

— Dennis Thompson, owner of Gypsy Gold Farm, who went out of his way to allow me to photograph Gypsy King.

— Peg and Jack Stockbridge, owners of Enchanted Acres, for their kind hospitality and efforts while I portrayed Sharlamane, Evening Victory, Soldier, and Felipe de Sourie.

— Kristen DeLuca, owner of Escudero.

My gratitude to: Jim Megargee and all the staff at MV Labs, for their great care in processing my film; Billy Collins, U.S. Poet Laureate, for my book's poetic title; Charlene St. Sauveur, for her brilliant insights about this book; Judy Reynolds, for always being there for me when I needed a friend's advice; David Jepson; and all the many people who assisted me during the process of making this book.

And, of course, I also wish to pay tribute to my team at Barnes and Noble, without whose expertise this book would not be what it is: Michael Fragnito, who tenaciously stuck with this project and forced me to surpass myself; Susan Lauzau, for her conscientious coordination of the entire project and her attentiveness to detail; Jeff Batzli, for his artistic vision; and Richela Morgan and Karen Matsu Greenberg, for achieving such remarkable reproductions of my photographs.

PLATE 78

A BARNES & NOBLE BOOK

Photographs © 2004 Juliet van Otteren

Text © 2004 Alan Lightman

Foreword © 2004 Jane Goodall

ISBN 0-7607-5927-8

Design by Stacey May

Color separations by North Market Street Graphics

Printed and bound in Singapore by CS Graphics

1 3 5 7 9 10 8 6 4 2

Photographer's Note

I began taking pictures of horses two years ago simply because I love them. Having ridden most of
my life, I wanted to be around them again, but differently. This time I wanted to listen to what they
were saying and record their innermost feelings with my camera.

To create the images included in this book, I spent endless hours studying these amazing creatures in
the privacy of my darkroom. I hope that these photographs will help people to better understand the
infinite complexity of horses' emotionality and allow them to better communicate with these intelligent
and sensitive beings.

The horses I photographed for this book were in no way harmed or forced to do anything they did not
want to do or that did not come naturally to them. They wore no bridles and were simply responding
to a communicative process that was born out of mutual respect.

For more information about Juliet van Otteren, please visit her website: www.JulietvanOtteren.com.